BLAMING ISLAM

BLAMING ISLAM

John R. Bowen

A Boston Review Book

THE MIT PRESS Cambridge, Mass. London, England

MIT Press books may be purchased at special quantity discounts
for business or sales promotional use. For information, please
email special_sales@mitpress.mit.edu or write to Special Sales
Department, The MIT Press, 55 Hayward Street, Cambridge, MA
02142.

This book was set in Adobe Garamond by *Boston Review*
and was printed and bound in the United States of America.

Library of Congress Cataloging-in-Publication Data

Bowen, John Richard, 1951–
Blaming Islam / John R. Bowen.
   p.   cm. — (A Boston review book)
Includes bibliographical references.
ISBN 978-0-262-01758-9 (hardcover : alk. paper)
1. Islam—United States—Public opinion. 2. Muslims—United
States. 3. Islamic law—United States. 4. Islamic law—Great
Britain. 5. Islamophobia. 6. Conservatism—United States. I.
Title.
BP67.U6B69   2012
305.6'97091821—dc23

2011049219

10   9   8   7   6   5   4   3   2   1

To Charles Caruson

CONTENTS

PREFACE

FOR THE LAST TEN YEARS, I HAVE BEEN WORK-
ing with Muslims and non-Muslims, scholars and ordinary people, politicians and public figures, mainly
in Europe and North America. Sometimes I focus on
Muslims' efforts to reinterpret the Islamic tradition,
sometimes on non-Muslims' apprehensions about
such a project. In France I wrote first on the fears
underpinning efforts to ban Islamic scarves from
schools, and then about Muslims' social and intellectual projects to adapt to France. Now I find my-
self in the same back-and-forth in Britain and the
United States. In each case, misunderstandings feed
suspicion and hatred. My preoccupation with this
dangerous causal chain lies behind the present slim

volume. Hence the central thrust: to demonstrate that certain misapprehensions fueling fear of Islam are just that: misapprehensions.

None of this is to deny the existence of cruelty, terrorism, and patriarchy in the world, among Muslims as well as among Hindus, Christians, and atheists. But pointing these things out in the case of Islam—an amplified industry—threatens to drown out those who wish to point to the ordinary, reasonable nature of the life projects of most Muslims and of their understandings of their faith. Let this modest work be one effort to clear away some dangerously scruffy brush so that more fine-grained portraits of Islam can survive.

Had it not been for the continued encouragement of Deborah Chasman and Joshua Cohen, editors of *Boston Review*, I would not have written the articles that gave rise to this volume, much less the book itself. We need many more ways to bridge academic research and public writing, and Deb and Josh are leading that struggle. Simon Waxman's heroic editing completes the picture.

My final acknowledgment reaches back to my high school years, where Charles Caruson taught me that argument needed to be put to the service of the social good, and that, for it to work, it needed to be good argument.

Introduction:
Finding an Enemy

AT ANY ONE MOMENT IN WESTERN HISTORY, some people have been targeted for broad-based hatred: Jews, Catholics, Protestants, Africans, Slavs, Gypsies, homosexuals, and, unfortunately, so forth. Today the primary targets of hate are Muslims. Why there need be targets is beyond the scope of this book, although Freud had something to say on the subject, as did the Frankfurt theorists. Anthropologists have pointed to ways human societies work by opposition, often bipolar opposition, us versus them, on scales ranging from feuding tribes to warring nation-states.

When a particular narrative of us versus them circulates widely, it can be used to dehumanize huge segments of humanity. Pogroms in Russia and genocide in Europe were fuelled by the poisonous *Protocols of the Elders of Zion*, which later found a second life in parts of the Muslim world. Communism and anti-Communism, twinned for decades, wound much of the newly postcolonial world into a web of intrigue and oppression. But after the fall of the Soviet Union there was an opening for a new them, a new enemy. Islam fit the bill.

A few academics gave "Islam versus the West" a new guise and some respectability, expressed most famously in Samuel Huntington's *The Clash of Civilizations* (1996), with its odd notion that the Chinese and the Muslims would make common ground against us. Well before 9/11, anti-Islamic sentiment also gained popularity in the United States through evangelical Protestant preaching. In parts of Europe it was inflamed by broad backlashes against the growing presence of Muslim immigrants. The attacks on 9/11 seemed to confirm the idea that Islam and the West were at war, as did the July 7, 2005 bombings in Britain and the Dutch filmmaker Theo van

Gogh's 2004 murder by a Moroccan immigrant in Amsterdam.

All along the way, it has at times been electorally expedient to blame Islam for a range of social ills. In most of Europe as in the United States, a new far-right populism has been gaining ground, and skilful politicians of the more moderate right have sought to reclaim some of those votes by joining in condemning Islam and the elites who supposedly coddled it. Attacks on Islam go hand in hand with attacks on multicultural politics in Europe and on liberal politicians in the United States. Populism is a broad church.

The drumbeat of anti-Islam propaganda can lead to sharp social divisions and violent actions. The most shocking recent example came on July 22, 2011, when Anders Behring Breivik opened fire on youth members of the Norwegian Labor Party, killing 69 teenagers, and bombed government buildings in Oslo, killing eight others. Breivik had written a long set of statements espousing hatred for all that he saw as destroying a properly Norwegian way of life.

Among his most despised targets were Islam and the multicultural politics of the elite. For years he had drenched himself in the writings of far-right, anti-Islam activists from the United States and Europe, and he planned his killing spree as a way of saving Europe from Islam. Anti-Islam writings do not explain his actions, but it is difficult to imagine those actions in the absence of such writings.[1]

More mundane but also disturbing are the local manifestations of widespread anti-Islam sentiment in the United States. In 2010 some residents of Murfreesboro, Tennessee protested plans by their Muslim neighbors to build a new mosque.[2] Frustrated when their city council approved the project, they launched a lawsuit claiming that the new mosque would bring more Muslims to the area, paving the way for sharia law. They were convinced that this was already happening elsewhere in America: "it's creeping in," said Sally Wall, a real estate agent who backed the lawsuit. The suit failed, despite the efforts of the prosecutor to prove that Islam was not a religion because it advocated oppressing and torturing women. An unsuccessful Republican congressional candidate joined the protest, others urged local contractors to boycott the project, and someone torched the construction equipment.

Murfreesboro shows us both the problem and the solution. Ignorant claims (sharia is already here, Muslims whip their womenfolk) comforted those who searched for a way to justify their unease at seeing headscarves on the street. Those claims fueled hatred and violence. But others in the town staged counter-protests, upholding constitutional rights to religious freedom. Moreover, the judge in the lawsuit, also a local man, ruled that the claims about creeping sharia had no legal relevance and that Muslims had the same right to worship as did those of other faiths. The mosque could go ahead. (As this book goes to press, the mosque's supporters are still raising money and looking for a contractor.)

What can we learn from this story? Three things. First, ideas have consequences. Publicly proclaiming false ideas about Muslims and Islam reinforces existing fears and can produce hatred and even violence. We know that ideology can lead ordinary people to commit awful crimes they otherwise would not have contemplated: German soldiers shooting prisoners, Khmer Rouge followers killing villagers, or Rwandans killing their neighbors. Second, people don't like to voyage out of their comfort zone. Those who feel upset when they see a mosque will easily accept arguments that explain or justify their discomfort. Third, laws and constitutional principles provide the best bulwark against hate speech, but they require consistent interpretation and vigorous enforcement. We must fight intolerance, even if it masquerades as literate, reasonable argument, and we must do so on the basis of shared principles.

In these chapters, I examine four theses that shape current fear-mongering about Islam in the West: that European governments have followed multiculturalist policies that have prevented Muslims from integrating; that in any case Muslim immigrants will remain apart from and opposed to the West; that the danger of all these trends is best seen in Britain, where super-multiculturalism has allowed sharia to become law; and that sharia is creeping into U.S. law thanks to inattentive judges. Each thesis is false.

At the heart of their arguments are basic errors in reasoning. In Chapter 1 I highlight how political leaders targeting "multiculturalism" confuse the social facts of cultural diversity, claims about state immigration policies, and normative political theories. Criticizing multiculturalism is attractive because it is more widely acceptable than is directly criticizing Islam. Realizing this, some politicians on the right have made a faulty reading of recent history part of their electoral campaigns.

Prominent anti-Islam writers in the United States argue that Europe is the central arena in the conflict over the future of the West. In Chapter 2 I argue that this fear-mongering about Muslims taking over Europe is based on the erroneous idea that all members of a group—Muslims in this case—think and act alike.

In Chapter 3 I focus on the case of Britain, to which American anti-Islam writers and politicians point as the place where sharia has most infiltrated legal and social life, as the worst case of multiculturalism gone awry. Britain does indeed have the most extensive network of sharia tribunals, nonlegal bodies that, much like North American Jewish tribunals, grant religious divorces and answer questions about religious obligations. And, as in the United States, these bodies raise important issues about whether and how civil courts should take account of what occurs in religious tribunals. In chapter 4 I discuss unwarranted anxieties surrounding sharia in the United States, inspired in part by false perceptions of how sharia works across the pond.

In debunking these four theses, I examine claims made by public actors (politicians, authors, ministers) about Islam and Muslims, claims that create a climate of fear and suspicion and that are founded on misreadings of our own institutions as much as on misunderstandings of Muslims. But in our everyday lives, many of us living in the United States or Europe impute religious motivations to actions of Muslims where we would be loath to do so vis-à-vis people of other faiths. Imagine that we read a statement of the form: "Muslims now constitute X percent of the prison population." We might interpret this statement in different ways. Some of us might infer that Islam is at the root of the problem. Others would argue that the Muslims in question are poor, and that poverty is to blame. We would probably say that, as long as it was true, the original statement was a factual statement, unproblematic in itself.

Now imagine that we read the statement: "Christians now constitute X percent of the prison population." Quite a few Americans and Europeans would object to putting the matter in that way, arguing—rightly, I think—that those in prison are not there because they are Christian but because of some other feature of their lives and that it is wrong to suggest that their religious beliefs are somehow responsible.

This is also how we should be reacting to the first statement, the "purely factual" statement about Muslims.

Over the past 50 years most of us have had to rethink how we speak in everyday life. We have recalibrated the ways we refer to women, men, members of racial and ethnic minorities, people of other faiths, and so on. We have learned that "just joking" doesn't cut it, that everyday habits of speaking and passively listening sustain prejudice of all sorts. Regarding Islam and Muslims, we are just at the start of this recalibration. It may help to begin by clearing out some of the misconceptions. That is the idea behind this book.

1

Europeans Against Multiculturalism

MISREADING THE RECENT PAST SEEMS TO BE AN election strategy shared by a number of leading European politicians. The far right is gathering strength across Europe, and, in efforts to capture its supporters, some center-right leaders are blaming the supposed multicultural policies of the past for a range of current ills. German Chancellor Angela Merkel led off in October 2010 by claiming that multiculturalism "has failed and failed utterly." She was echoed the following February by French President Nicolas Sarkozy and British Prime Minister David Cameron. All three were late to the game, though: for years, the Dutch right has been bashing supposedly multicultural policies.[1]

Despite the shared rhetoric, it is difficult to discern a common target for these criticisms. Cameron aimed at an overly tolerant attitude toward extremist Islam, Merkel at the slow pace of Turkish integration, and Sarkozy at Muslims who pray in the street. But while it is hard to know what exactly the politicians of Europe mean when they talk about multiculturalism, one thing we do know is that the issues they raise—real or imagined—have complex historical roots that have little to do with ideologies of cultural difference. Blaming multiculturalism may be politically useful because of its populist appeal, but it is also politically dangerous because it attacks "an enemy within": Islam and Muslims. Moreover, it misreads history. An intellectual corrective may help to diminish its malign impact.

Political criticisms of multiculturalism confuse three objects. One is the changing cultural and religious landscape of Europe. Postwar France and Britain encouraged immigration of willing workers from former colonies; Germany drew on its long-standing ties with Turkey for the same purpose. Beginning in the 1960s, new African and Asian immigrants, many of them Muslims, travelled throughout Western Europe to seek jobs or, particularly in the 1990s and thereafter, to seek political refuge. As a result, one sees mosques where there once were only churches and hears Arabic and Turkish where once there were only dialects of German, Dutch, or Italian. The first object, then, is the social fact of cultural and religious diversity, of multicultural and multi-religious everyday life: the emergence in Western Europe of the kind of social diversity that has long been a matter of pride in the United States.[2]

The second object—suggested by Cameron's phrase "state multiculturalism"—concerns the policies each of these countries has used to handle new residents. By the 1970s Western European governments realized that the new workers and their families were staying put, so the host countries tried out a number of strategies to integrate immigrants into their adopted societies. Policymakers all realized that they would need to find what later came to be called "reasonable accommodations" with the needs of the new communities: for mosques and schools, job training, instruction in the host-country language. These were pragmatic efforts; they neither aimed to assimilate the newcomers nor to preserve spatial or cultural separation. Some of these policies eventually were termed "multicultural" because they involved recognizing ethnic community structures or allowing the use of Arabic or Turkish in schools. But they all were designed to encourage integration: to bring new groups in while acknowledging the obvious facts of linguistic, social, cultural, and religious difference.

The third object that multiculturalism's critics confusingly mix together with the other two is a set of normative theories of multiculturalism, each of which attempts to mark out a way to take account of cultural and religious diversity from a particular philosophical point of view. Although ideas of multiculturalism do shape public debates in Britain (as they do in North America), they do so much less in continental Europe.

Politicians err when they claim that normative ideas of multiculturalism shape the social fact of cultural and religious diversity: such diversity would be present with or without a theory to cope with it. Nor have European state policies regarding integration and immigration been shaped by multicultural philosophies. Quite to the contrary, each European country has followed its own well-traveled national pathways for dealing with diversity. Methods originally designed to accommodate sub-national religious blocs within each country are now being adapted and applied to Muslim immigrants. Far from being newfangled, misguided policies of multiculturalism, these distinct strategies represent the continuation of long-standing, nation-specific ways of recognizing and managing diversity.

Consider the case of Germany. Merkel's claims were perhaps the least weighty, but her words point to a growing conviction among some Germans that Muslim immigrants are inassimilable. Merkel's attack was as vague as it was opportunistic. She regretted that the German "tendency had been to say, 'let's adopt the multicultural concept and live happily side by side, and be happy to be living with each other'" and concluded that this attitude had not produced results, as if she had thereby identified policies that could be changed. Her real meaning was made clear by the presence of Horst Seehofer next to her on the podium. Seehofer, the Bavarian state premier and Merkel's coalition partner, had been issuing calls to curtail immigration, and Merkel was wooing his followers.

Merkel's speech followed a series of anti-Muslim public statements by high-placed German officials. In June 2010 then-Bundesbank member Thilo Sarrazin published a book in which he accused Muslim immigrants of lowering the intelligence of German society. Although he was censured for his views and dismissed from his central bank position, the book proved popular, and polls suggested that Germans were sympathetic to the thrust of his arguments. One poll showed a third of Germans believed the country was "overrun by foreigners." That March, Finance Minister Wolfgang Schäuble had waded in to say that Germany had been mistaken to let in so many Turkish workers in the 1960s because they had not integrated into society.

At least the finance minister pointed to a real German policy, one that encouraged low-paid laborers to relocate to the country and rebuild it. But Merkel's notion that the German government had promoted a *multikulti* society (as distinct from celebrating the colorful Kreuzberg neighborhood of Berlin or a star Turkish player on the German soccer team) ignores the brunt of German immigration policy, which, until 2000, denied citizenship to the Turkish workers, their children, and their grandchildren. In other words, the government and many, perhaps most, Germans had *not* hoped, as Merkel claimed, that everyone would live side by side. Rather, the hope was that "they" would just pack up and leave.[3]

In this sense Germany has largely followed its longer-term policies for dealing with diversity: German federal and state governments have historically denied that immigration could be of value and maintained a policy of limiting citizenship only to those who could demonstrate German descent. But Germany also has sought to apply a model that has long been used to support Christian and Jewish groups, one in which such groups can be recognized as public corporations, eligible for state funding. A proposed Islamic public corporation would have the legal status to obtain government funding for mosques and would serve as a legitimate overseer of materials selected for Islamic religious education. This promising policy goal, not yet achieved, would recognize and support Islam in accordance with long-standing German principles governing religious diversity, not on grounds of multiculturalism.

IN CONTRAST TO GERMANY, BRITAIN HAS promoted multiculturalism as an explicit policy, but not in those domains where Cameron denounced it. In his February 2011 speech, Cameron blamed multiculturalism for creating spatial divisions and fomenting terrorism. "Under the doctrine of state multiculturalism," he claimed, "we have encouraged different cultures to live separate lives, apart from each other and apart from the mainstream." Left apart, some have submitted to extremism, he argued, and some of those extremists have in turn carried bombs in the name of Islam. His solution was threefold: ensure that any organization asking for public money subscribes to doctrines of universal rights and encourages integration, keep extremists from reaching students and prisoners, and ensure that everyone learns English.

As a diagnosis of homegrown terrorism, the speech fell short. The British bombers principally responsible for the 2005 attacks in London knew the English language and English people very well. Mohammad Sidique Khan, believed to be the leader of the bombing plot, was recalled as a "highly Westernized" man who grew up in Leeds and attended university there. Shehzad Tanweer, another of the bombers, had a similar background. According to the official report on the bombings, both men had developed jihadist convictions in Pakistan.

If these and other "homegrown" terrorists have problems feeling at home in Britain, it is not because they remain in their separate cultures but because they become isolated individuals without a social or cultural base. In otherwise-distinct analyses of European jihadists, French political scientist Olivier Roy and American counterterrorism expert Marc Sageman each paint a picture of young men who suffer from a lack of ties with others in their communities. Roy calls them "deterritorialized"; Sageman describes a "bunch of guys" who find themselves without opportunities and without acceptance in their European homes, and end up traveling abroad to seek out extremists. Hardly walled off in enclaves in Bradford (or Hamburg), they are free-floating, perfect speakers of English (or German) who feel rejected by the people and institutions around them.[4]

Cameron used his speech to argue for his "Big Society"—policies of state divestment from welfare predicated on the belief that if people have to work together to survive they will gain a stronger sense of being British. But whatever the merits of this approach to British social ills, it has little to offer individuals who already consider themselves discarded by their neighbors.

So Cameron got it wrong when it comes to home-grown terrorism. What did he have in mind when he spoke of "state multiculturalism"? Multicultural policies in Britain today mainly concern how state schools handle their diverse clientele: teaching cultural and religious studies curricula, offering halal meals to Muslim pupils, accepting or refusing various forms of religious dress. Behind these specific policies is the notion, generally accepted in Britain and deriving from Imperial strategies of rule and Commonwealth policies of entry and settlement, that the cultural and religious traditions of each pupil should be positively recognized. These politics find one salient expression in a white paper commissioned from the political theorist Bhikhu Parekh, whose 2000 book, *Rethink-*

ing Multiculturalism, asks: In a multicultural society, how should the state balance legitimate claims to diversity with the need to "foster a strong sense of unity and common belonging among its citizens"?[5] This is precisely Cameron's concern, but Parekh voices it as a justification *for* educational multiculturalism. He argues that recognizing the traditions held by religious and ethnic communities through multicultural school curricula provides a psychologically sound basis on which to construct an inclusive national identity. (His view comes close to claims made by another political theorist, Will Kymlicka, who draws mainly on North American examples to argue that maintaining cultural heritage is of psychosocial importance in the development of a liberal citizen.)

There is indeed controversy in Britain about schooling and the isolation of cultural minorities. However, the spatial segregation of immigrant communities was a product of South Asian settlement patterns in Britain in the 1960s and '70s, not state multiculturalism. When men (and, later, families) moved from Pakistan and Bangladesh to Britain, they brought whole lineages and villages along with them, reproducing their old linguistic and religious networks in urban British neighborhoods. The result was a chasm separating Asian and white communities, and in some cities this absence of interaction and understanding spiralled into hatred and unrest. In the spring and summer of 2001, riots pitted Asians against whites in the northern cities of Oldham, Burnley, and Bradford. Today, these cities remain highly segregated. Their schools reflect, and exacerbate, the problem. Pupils remain sorted into largely white and largely Pakistani or Bangladeshi schools. As one head teacher at a 92 percent Pakistani primary school said in a report released on the tenth anniversary of the riots, "Some of our children could live their lives without meeting someone from another culture until they go to high school or even the workplace."

The combination of religion and schooling contributes to this segregation, but not in the way that

Cameron's speech suggests: it's not just Muslims who've cut themselves off from the rest of society. Across Britain a large percentage of children go to schools that only admit students who regularly attend a Catholic or an Anglican church. In sharply segregated Oldham, 40 percent of secondary schools are of this type, and they draw from a largely white population. This religious divide is increasing due to the addition to the school scene of state-supported "faith academies," mainly Church of England and Catholic schools. Whereas in the United States this degree of government support for religiously exclusive schools would be judged as excessive entanglement of the state with religion, British ideas of public life start from the premise that religious communities are legitimate and socially important sources of citizen education, and thus deserve state aid.

So if British state multiculturalism exists in 2012, it is in broadly accepted principles about the role of state support in promoting diverse kinds of schools. These policies can have segregating effects, but they are also current Tory policies. Cameron and his party don't like to bring them up as examples of failed multiculturalism, though; they are not in the business of attacking Christian schools.

On the whole, then, it seems that accommodation of immigrants in Britain has taken the usual course for that nation. The methods applied to distinct religious groups that predate Islam on the Isles—Catholics, Jews, Quakers, and others—have been extended to the newest arrivals.

Cameron's policy proposals were on a wholly different topic: he paid special attention to reducing the degree of toleration afforded Islamic groups with extreme views. Here one might join with the prime minister in finding that certain Islamic groups ought to have their public activities curtailed. The most frequently cited example is the Hizb ut-Tahrir, a group that rejects participation in British politics and urges British Muslims to prepare themselves for the coming of the Islamic state, to be created somewhere in the world in the not-too-distant future. But whatever one might think about whether this group should be allowed to spread its views freely, this question has nothing to do with the validity of recognizing cultural diversity. Rather, it concerns the degree to which the state ought to allow extreme or intolerant public speech, the same issue that arose from the Danish cartoons controversy and that regularly figures in laws against Holocaust denial.

These British attacks on multiculturalism thus muddle the issues in ways that target Mulsims and past governments. The attacks are politically useful to a conservative leadership, but they get in the way of clear thinking about serious problems of employment, declining social services, and lack of hope among many young people.

ALTHOUGH FRENCH PRESIDENT NICOLAS SARkozy attacked *le multiculturalisme*, more often French politicians use the term "communalism" (*communautarisme*). This refers not to the North American philosophy of communitarianism, although that takes its lumps sometimes, but to everyday practices and attitudes that are thought of as rejecting "living together" in favor of "living side by side." Usually Britain is the example of all this, though of late the French have been blaming themselves for the deficiency as well.

But communalism is no more precise an object of denunciation than is multiculturalism. In 2010 Interior Minister Claude Guéant said that high unemployment among those who come to France from outside the European Union proves "the failure of communalisms" because those immigrants tend to clump together by culture and doing so keeps them from getting jobs. He acknowledged that people chose where to live, that the state did not put them there, but argued, "We have gone too long in letting people group together in communities." Guéant suggests that what has been going on is a state multiculturalism of inaction, but he doesn't specify how the state could break up existing communities.[6]

On the same day, French journalists were analyzing the American "Galleon affair," a case of financial fraud involving financiers from India, as itself an instance of communalism, because these men, who held degrees from Harvard and Wharton and worked at Goldman Sachs and McKinsey, had common national origins. Contrary to Guéant's claims, these immigrants who clumped together got great jobs. Apparently communalism of one sort is the key to success, albeit illicit, while communalism of another sort explains high unemployment rates. A cynic might add that if working in small incestuous groups defines communalism, then France—with its unusually small set of industrialists serving on interlocking boards of major companies, its exclusive school system, and its class-endogamous marriage practices designed to preserve the elite—is among the most communalist of nations.

In any case, France has never undertaken state multiculturalism. Although some officials have decried the politics of the "right to a difference" that marked several years at the beginning of François Mitterrand's presidency in the 1980s, those politics could hardly be called multicultural.[7] Some instruction in "languages of origin" was provided, but this was intended to facilitate the eventual "return" of immigrants and their children. Other sources of aid provided tutoring and training, and current policies direct additional money to school districts with large numbers of pupils "in difficulty." At the same time, the French state has provided free language classes to immigrants, assistance to groups seeking to build mosques, and practical accommodations to allow the preparation of halal meat in abattoirs. State support for and control of religious groups is, despite the rhetoric of strict state-religion separation, a long-term feature of French policy. More than a century after France's 1905 law of church-state separation, the state pays for the upkeep of older religious buildings, gives tax breaks to religious groups, and hires teachers for private religious schools (most of them Catholic).[8] These centuries-old Gallican policies of supervising religions enjoy broad political support; they have nothing to do with *le multiculturalisme*.

BLAMING MULTICULTURALISM FOR SOCIAL ILLS IS a Dutch national sport. Yet the Netherlands has never pursued policies designed to preserve and celebrate cultural difference. Instead it has pursued two distinct sets of policies, with distinct pasts. One is a century old and has aimed at maintaining religious and political peace; the other dates from the 1970s and has aimed at achieving the integration of minorities.[9]

The first set of policies reflects the enduring Dutch preference for compromise, often referred to as the "polder model"—a reference to working together to build dykes, a watery equivalent to American "barn-raisings." Historically this meant that people refrained from criticizing others, including unassimilated immigrants. Dutch cultural practices favored the unofficial continuation of a multicultural social reality, where people were free to continue to speak their own languages, worship in their own ways, and so forth. This kind of "live and let live" social habit was developed as the Dutch solution to the religious conflicts that characterized a period of relatively intense religious belief and practice in the nineteenth century. It gave rise to a quasi-official model of "pillars": religious networks and institutions within which each Dutch person was presumed to remain.

This social conception of keeping the religious and political peace by structuring society around these pillars subtended policies of creating and financing religious schools. Although the pillar structure had effectively dissolved before major Muslim immigration was underway in the 1970s and '80s, a psychological residue persisted, dictating that each religious group should ignore the particularities of the other. Far from accepting or recognizing the other's validity, this attitude promoted a bare tolerance, civic acceptance of Catholics, Protestants, and, for that matter, gays and pot-smokers. Condemnation was constrained to the home or the pulpit. So while Dutch policies and norms favored a diverse society, they took no part in what is today thought of as multiculturalism, with its efforts to reach beyond toleration toward appreciation. And, for that matter, these policies concerned homegrown religious and political diversity and echoed the long history of European religious wars, not recent labor migration.

But after labor migration was in full swing, successive Dutch governments developed a series of policies aimed at promoting the advancement of minorities through a number of measures, including providing schoolteachers who spoke their languages (principally Arabic and Turkish), appointing local councils to advise the government on how best to foster integration, and providing funds for additional tutoring and support at schools heavily attended by the children of immigrants. By the end of the twentieth century, these policies had been changed to focus more on skills training and teaching in Dutch. But while the specific efforts have changed over the course of the past 40 years, the policy goal has always been to promote integration. In the Netherlands, as in France, financial aid was targeted at schools with many poor students, who happened to descend from recent immigrants.

Attacks on these policies have combined populist anti-elitism with denunciations of Islam. In 1991 parliamentary opposition leader Frits Bolkestein criticized the government for failing to defend Western values of free speech and equality against Islamic views. He attacked the political elite and their habits of papering over differences (the polder model) rather than standing up for Enlightenment values against the Islam of the Ayatollahs. A rising class of populist politicians seconded this critique, among them the right-wing and openly gay Pim Fortuyn and the anti-Islam campaigners Ayaan Hirsi Ali and Geert Wilders. Their attacks on Islam were also political appeals against the elites, made in order to curry favor with the forgotten working class. Polder politics, elite domination, and Islam were the common enemy, and the refusal of the leading classes to denounce non-Dutch and anti-Enlightenment Islamic values was the major evidence that things had gone wrong. As in France, this admonition has been heard on the left and the right, from Social Democrats as well as from Wilders's far-right

Party for Freedom. It reflects a cultural nationalism that can appeal to the old-style populism of the right or to the universalism of the left.[10]

In life and, after his murder in 2002, in death, Fortuyn narrowed the criticism of multiculturalism so that it became an attack on Islamic intolerance of sexual diversity and, in particular, of gay lifestyles. Fortuyn personified a secularist, sexually open, and "tolerant" Dutch identity, against which Islam and Muslims could easily be targeted as the pre-Enlightenment other. In no other country has the issue of tolerating gays become so central and so salient a part of the critique of Islam. This line of attack was powerful because it also was a critique of older Dutch ways of doing politics and thinking about sexuality. Throughout most of the twentieth century, most Dutch people held religious views about homosexuality and women's rights that were not too different from those now ascribed to Muslims by their opponents. Attacking Islam can be a psychologically useful way of reworking one's own heritage.

Ironically, the current focus on Islam per se—Wilders has compared the Qur'an to *Mein Kampf* and seeks to have it banned in the Netherlands—has distracted the far right from policies about minority achievement and language learning. The focus now is on the acceptability in the Enlightenment West of the pre-Enlightenment Muslim. And yet the right continues to attack Dutch multiculturalism because it remains rhetorically useful to link the cultural critique of religion to a populist critique of past elites.

BLAMING MULTICULTURALISM, THEN, IS USEFUL because it is both vague and misdirected. It would be hard for Cameron to acknowledge that British racism, immigration trajectories, foreign policy, and faith-based schools have made major contributions toward minority isolation; much harder than it is to say: we got it wrong, now let's get it right, let's all be British. Islam provides a soft target for aspiring cultural nationalists. It is easier for Sarkozy and Marine Le Pen of the right-wing French National Front to decry Muslims praying in the street than it is to make room for adequate mosques. And across Europe, it is easier to point to the irresponsible statement of a foreign imam and say that Islam is the problem than to figure out how Muslims, like practicing Catholics and Jews before them, might best construct the cultural and religious institutions they need to be at ease in their new (and not so new) countries.

One can, and should, refute these misdiagnoses and at the same time give due credit to policies promoting integration within each of these societies. Speaking the language of the country and gaining job skills are keys to becoming a productive citizen. France made free French courses part of its "integration contract" in 2003; with its 2005 Immigration Act, Germany began providing free German lessons to people granted work visas. When most Islamic religious officials are recent immigrants, it makes good sense to offer them instruction in the language, law, and politics of their new country of residence. These are policies of integration rather than assimilation;

they are perfectly consistent with the promotion of equal respect for all religions and cultures.

Blaming multiculturalism ties the package together: it discredits a foreign element—Islam—and it identifies the fifth column that let it in, those past proponents of multiculturalism. That it misreads history is beside the point. It makes for effective, albeit irresponsible, populist politics. And that is precisely why it must be corrected.

2

*Misreading Muslim
Immigration*

THE CRITIQUES OF MULTICULTURALISM ARE GEN-
erally polite. Quite different is the body of work de-
crying Islam. If you wish to read a book along these
lines in Europe, you have many to choose from. The
dominant style on the continent is the memoir that
recounts the horrific experiences of a Muslim (or for-
merly Muslim) woman in her Islamic milieu. *Infidel*
and *The Caged Virgin*, by Ayaan Hirsi Ali, are the most
familiar in this genre. The best-selling French titles
speak for themselves: *Dishonored*; *Mutilated*; *The Sold
Ones* and *The Fatiha* (both on forced marriages); *Disfig-
ured*; *Souad, Burned Alive*; and *Latya, Her Face Stolen*.

   Europe's anti-Islam sentiment may be expressed
most visibly in memoirs because Europeans have been

reticent to condemn Islam—or religion more generally—outright. Americans, however, seem to prefer a less subtle approach. In the United States, alongside the autobiographies, we find direct attacks on Islam as a false religion or as a threat to our fundamental values—a threat that has already overrun Europe and is now heading this way. We find this kind of warning in Bruce Bawer's *While Europe Slept: How Radical Islam is Destroying the West from Within*, or his *Surrender: Appeasing Islam, Sacrificing Freedom*; also in Brigitte Gabriel's *They Must Be Stopped*; and Mark Steyn's *America Alone: The End of the World as We Know It*.

Perhaps these books are innocent, less about an animus against Islam than an expression of Americans' secret delight in knocking weak-kneed French and English politicians. Or maybe we simply prefer displacing our anxiety about Islam from the nice Pakistani surgeon next door onto jihadists invading European cities.

But these cheerful interpretations do not do justice to the books' somber tones and striking thematic consistency, shared with many like-minded Web sites. Islam, they argue, has shocked Europeans, the shock comes from Islamic values, and the clash is unlikely to subside. These three themes—Islamic shock, value conflict, and unending struggle—evoke Huntington's *Clash of Civilizations*, but with added urgency and vivid examples.

We need to take this argument seriously and understand what is wrong with it. And—to cut right to the chase—it is wrong on every detail that matters.

CONSIDER FIRST THE IDEA OF AN ISLAMIC SHOCK: that Islamic immigrants have disrupted European life in ways completely unlike previous waves of immigrants. On its face, the argument is valid: before World War II, most workers coming to Western Europe were European Christians (usually Catholics), who looked more or less like the natives. By contrast, the workers coming into Germany, Britain, France, and elsewhere after 1945 included more non-Europeans than ever before, mostly rural Muslims from

Africa or Asia. Post-1970s we have been witnessing a third wave of people from Africa and Asia trying to make their way into Europe's supranational regime of immigration, the Schengen Area, a zone comprising 25 countries. For many securely inside the Area, Europe may seem a fortress with its Maginot line at Calais (confusingly, Britain is outside the Area) and its porous points on the shores of Mayotte and the walls around the Spanish North African enclave cities of Ceuta and Melilla. Storming the walls, swimming the seas, or trekking across borders come thousands of refugees and asylum seekers, along with people claiming family-reunification rights, people working without proper papers, people on the way, perhaps, to having proper papers—all immigrants less welcome than earlier ones but pressing to get a toehold on the Old Continent.

There are real differences among these three historical streams of immigrants. And the Islamic character of much of the second and third waves has indeed bothered many Europeans. In response, we see mayors refusing to allow the construction of—and, a few times, razing—mosques; landlords refusing to rent to Muslims; controversies over headscarves; and in Switzerland, minarets singled out as signs of "Islamism." All these recurrent actions testify to the shock felt by many, not to mention the rhetoric of far-right political parties. For those not on the far right, complaining of too many "immigrants" has been a common and relatively safe way of complaining of too much Islam.

But those who point to an "Islamic shock" are not just arguing that newer immigrants are different from older ones; they also argue that the new wave of immigration has been uniquely disruptive of a European "way of life." In this narrative, pre-Islamic immigration involved native white Europeans sharing the same values, going to the same churches, and welcoming new immigrants with their good hearts. This story is, it turns out, baloney. Yet even the most knowledgeable of the recent European-Islamic-threat writers, the journalist Christopher Caldwell in his

Reflections on the Revolution in Europe (2009), describes an undifferentiated Europe now besieged by Muslims.[1] Conveniently forgotten are centuries of religious wars, revolutions and counter-revolutions, attacks on Belgian and Italian immigrants to France, and, of course, culpability for the events of the early 1940s, in which good French and Dutch people joined good Germans in denouncing and arresting Jews and transporting them to death camps.

Lest we relegate those events to a distant past, we should ask how much serious reflection on the 1940s one hears from the Netherlands, say, or Norway (or Poland or . . .), or why it remains so difficult to extradite war criminals from Germany, or why old-style anti-Semitism (by hooligans, not Moroccans) remains so firmly entrenched in the European landscape.

The pertinence of these objections comes from the Burkean core of Caldwell's complaints, highlighted by his title. People, he argues, should not have to radically change their ways of life. But the massive arrival of Muslims has forced such changes, wrested quiet Europeans from their peaceful ways, and forced them to look at minarets next to their steeples. Yet when about one-third of French people freely admit to being racist, and Britons on camera casually compare Muslims to cockroaches, the conservative argument loses some of its bite. Perhaps some Europeans need a good jolt to confront the persistent racism that plagues the continent. It was not by calming troubled souls that the United States moved from centuries of slavery and Jim Crow to electing a black president. Confronting the American dilemma required a long fight for civil rights. Most of us think that we are a better society for it. Perhaps Europeans would take a comparable and proper pride in confronting the European dilemma, making good on their own premises and promises of social equality.

Caldwell's Burkean argument does not include new policies. Burke himself championed the gradual, English way of change over the abrupt French one, forgetting how much violence and intolerance accompanied even the Glorious Revolution. What then are the practical conclusions to be drawn from anti-Islamic Burkean sentiments? Europe is already a plural society. Do we send Muslim European citizens "back"?

As we saw in the last chapter, more common are calls to reverse the misguided "multiculturalist" policies that ostensibly engendered large Muslim populations in the first place. This is an odd argument, given that neither culture nor its multi-ness had anything to do with the arrival of the workers and their families. Workers came out of mutual economic self-interest. After World War II, European governments recruited workers (who happened to be mainly Muslims) to rebuild Europe. The governments placed these workers in lodgings away from the rest of the population. When the immigrants did not leave, and the recession of the 1970s made their presence less desirable, family reunification became the main argument for allowing new immigrants to settle legally in Europe; this remains the case today. Indeed, since the 1980s, legal migration by people who are Muslims is almost entirely due to Europeans obeying international legal requirements that people be allowed to lead a "normal family life."

Indeed, current laws and policies in most of Western Europe do not promote immigration, but mainly guarantee residents' legal rights. In Britain this means the right to wear religiously motivated dress to school and eat religiously required foods in the school canteen. In the Netherlands and France it means the right to have state support for religious schools that open their doors to anyone. These rights were won by earlier generations of Catholics and Protestants; they have nothing to do with naïve multiculturalist Islamophilia. While these legal rights are often challenged—by onerous language requirements in the Netherlands, or severe restrictions on family reunification in Italy—in principle, they are assured.

THE SECOND THESIS, ABOUT A CONFLICT OVER values, is similarly shaky. The central idea is that Muslim culture or religion (or both) have been disruptive not because of local prejudice but because Muslims do not share European commitments to universal values. The argument has nation-specific inflections: in the Netherlands, it often crystallizes around the Dutch tolerance for gay men versus Islamic intolerance of same; in Norway, around cases of forced marriage; in France, Belgium, and, most recently, Italy, around the oppression of women symbolized by a few hundred niqabs or burqas.

These arguments suffer shallow historical memory. As Paul Sniderman and Louk Hagendoorn remind us in their *When Ways of Life Collide* (2007), a generation ago those Dutch people who today vaunt their egalitarianism and their toleration of all lifestyles were authoritarian in family life and homophobic in public and in private.[2] A recent study found a rising number of young Dutch men who espouse attitudes of tolerance, but then attack gay men.[3] Nor have Europeans always been gender-equal. Two generations ago, French women were not able to vote and did not have the same rights to property as men, and Muslim women in much of the world had more avenues to gaining divorce than did most European women. Europeans, Africans, and Asians all have been moving gradually toward greater legal recognition of equal rights for women and men, and everywhere it has been a struggle.

Shallow historical memory is a problem, but perhaps the more insidious defect of these arguments is their reliance on block thinking, whereby the diversity of perspectives within a social group is collapsed into a single caricature. Today, in Europe and elsewhere, there is a widespread assumption that all Muslims think one way and all non-Muslims another. True, polls show that in relatively nonreligious Europe, Muslims are more likely than non-Muslims to be opposed to abortion, homosexuality, and suicide. According to a 2009 Gallup survey, in France 78 percent of the general public finds homosexuality morally acceptable, compared to 35 percent of French Muslims. We could also, however, compare Europeans with Americans on this question. A 2009

Pew study reported that 49 percent of Americans find homosexuality to be "morally wrong," that regular churchgoing means a greater likelihood of disapproval, and that American Protestants and American Muslims disapprove of homosexuality in equal measure—60 percent.[4] The gap is not between Islam and the West, but between people who are more religious and people who are less religious, whether Muslim or Christian.

WHAT ABOUT THE IDEA OF AN UNENDING STRUGGLE? Some of the Islam-versus-the-West folks claim that differences in civilization and religion between Islam and Europe will last because a fast-growing Muslim population is poised to take over European cities and establish political control in the name of a global *ummah*, or community. This argument disputes the notion that Muslim immigrants (and, a fortiori, their children) will do what most immigrants do: adapt. To the contrary, the argument says, multiculturalist—as opposed to assimilationist—policies isolate Muslims just as ummah TV is reaching youth with calls for jihad, and the new generations will continue to be motivated by radical Islam in all areas of their lives: they will plan families, build schools, and riot, all with Islamic political victory as their goal.

Proponents of this argument can point to Muslims growing up in Europe from the late 1980s on, who were more focused on Islam than their predecessors. That generation began to organize—using the opportunities and political styles characteristic of each host country—to achieve equal social, political, and religious rights. British Pakistanis and Bangladeshis organized local action committees and sharia councils (as we see in the next chapter), French North Africans formed national confederations of mosques, and rival factions of German Turks tried to reach the level of agreement required to form a public corporation and receive state aid.

In creating sharia councils, British Muslims began to look "separatist," and some do call for greater authority for sharia mediation. Against that British institutional background, a good number of younger Muslims called for governance "by sharia," whatever that might mean. French Muslims began to look "corporatist," as national organizations sought control over local mosque financing; everyone—Muslims included—calls for *laïcité* (secularity) to be applied equally. Throughout Europe, some Muslims developed ties with transnational groups: intellectual ties with the Muslim Brothers, spiritual ones with West African Sufi orders, financial ones with Gulf sheikhs.

In other words, these Islamic political actors have adapted to national ways and opportunities with more or less success: more in the cases of British, French, and Belgian Muslims, less in the cases of German, Dutch, and Swedish ones. The organizing that ostensibly proves Islamism in fact shows that these immigrants are following the examples of their predecessors. Like Catholics and Jews before them, Muslims build religious schools and associations—usually with external financial aid—and get involved in elections. In Britain, Bangladeshis and Pakistanis are more likely to vote than are other British citizens. This might look to some like evidence of Muslims trying to take political control, but political engagement seems to be accompanied by trust in government. The 2009 Gallup poll on Islam and integration found that Muslims in Germany and Britain had more confidence in the courts and the national governments than did the general German and British publics. (French Muslims had slightly less confidence in each.) In France, half of all Muslims supported the law most often cited there as anti-Islamic: the 2004 ban of Islamic headscarves from public schools. Muslims are adapting like everyone else and are divided like everyone else.[5]

Since European Muslims are working through national political structures, some of them become frustrated when those structures fail to make good on the promise of equal treatment. The most extreme response to this frustration is France's urban strife—the riots that began in late 2005 in some poor areas and rising everyday violence ever since. France's FBI, at the time called the Renseignements Généraux, analyzed the 2005 violence as "popular revolts" fueled by joblessness, family breakdown, and discrimination—an analysis with which *The Economist* concurred. If one assumes that Islam governs all antisocial acts committed by people with Arabic or Turkish last names, then the French authorities cannot be right. (This assumption leads Caldwell, for example, to make the surprising and unsupported conclusion that although the rioters may not have said they were rioting for religious reasons, in fact they were all fundamentalists who believed in Team Islam.)

Attempting to refute arguments about assimilation, anti-Muslim writers also assert that Muslims will continue to have high birth rates because the Prophet told them to and because it serves the Islamist strategy to conquer Europe. Anti-Muslim Web sites predict that in 2050 Europe will be half Muslim. Conservative pundits from Patrick Buchanan and Bernard Lewis to the commentators at the partisan Population Research Institute warn that Europe and Christianity will succumb to Islam because of differential birth rates. The now-viral "Muslim Demographics" video on YouTube tells viewers that France has 1.8 children per family but "Muslims, 8.1 children per family" and that "in just 39 years, France will be an Islamic Republic." (Both the BBC and the Web site Tiny Frog have assembled detailed rebuttals.)

Putting aside the faulty data—France does not even collect demographic data by religion—these arguments have two deficiencies. First, total fertility rates (TFR) are falling in many of the Muslim-majority countries sending people to Europe. In Morocco, for example, during the period 1985–2003 the TFR fell from 4.5 to 2.5 and is projected to fall to 1.9 by 2030–35, thus approximating European rates. (France currently has a TFR of 2.1.) For Muslim-majority countries taken as a whole, TFRs are projected to fall from 4.3 during 1990–95 to 2.3 in 2030–35, while TFR in developed, non-majority-Muslim countries will remain stable at 1.7.[6] Second, Muslim women born in European countries are doing precisely what demographers predict: having fewer children. Fertility rates for Muslim women born in European countries are declining quickly, heading toward rates for non-Muslim natives.[7] A recent Pew Research Forum study projects that the percentage of Muslims in Europe will grow from 6 percent in 2010 to 8 percent in 2030. The countries with the highest concentrations of Muslims will be France and Belgium, each with just over 10 percent.[8] We are far from the scary demographic projections.

But even if European Muslims are increasingly acting like other Europeans in the polling place and the bedroom, don't Islamic institutions—mosques and schools—feed the ranks of al Qaeda? A number of jihadists have come from Europe's cities, but as the counterterrorism expert Marc Sageman argues in *Leaderless Jihad* (2008), they were woefully un-educated in Islam and thus incapable of evaluating the jihadist arguments. "It follows," he writes, "that more religious education for these young men might have been beneficial." Developing centers of religious learning and teaching—as the governments of many European countries are committed to doing—will help spread more sophisticated understandings of Islam to the detriment of more superficial and radical ones.[9]

EUROPE WILL SURVIVE ITS CHANGING COMPOsition, as it has before. But the political shape of the Europe that emerges will depend on how European leaders frame the matter of citizenship. Europeans have some experience, not particularly rosy, of dividing people by religious affiliation and of making one group the scapegoat for all that ails them. A sequel probably will not lead to a happier end. Most European leaders—on the right and left—know this and in practice are seeking ways to build and broaden national institutions to include, on equal grounds, their Muslim citizens. (Their rhetoric often leans the other way, as we saw in the previous chapter.) They are supporting the creation of schools and mosques, debating the hard questions of sociability and religious freedom, and developing new ways of enforcing antidiscrimination laws. To be sure, some European political figures are rekindling old fires. Those of us on the other side of the Atlantic would do well to understand their constructive practical efforts rather than fanning the rhetorical flames.

3

*Sharia Is Not
the Law in England*

IN 2010 NASEERA, A MUSLIM WOMAN, approached a religious teacher near her London home. She wished to divorce her husband. She had grown up in England but married her cousin in Pakistan, a union arranged by their parents. They moved to England and later separated. Naseera was planning to file for a legal divorce in court, but she also wanted proof that she was divorced religiously in case she wished to remarry. The teacher referred her to London's Islamic Sharia Council, and in 2011, at one of their monthly meetings at the Regent's Park Mosque, the six Islamic scholars sitting as the Council took up her case.

Their first aim, as with Islamic judges in other countries, was to save the marriage. But, as is often the case, Naseera's husband had not answered their entreaties to come for a joint meeting. As a result they agreed to dissolve the marriage, and officially informed Naseera of their decision. With their letter, she would be able to remarry in a country practicing Islamic law, where a judge might ask for such a letter, or, should she remarry in England, she would be able to satisfy relatives and neighbors, and perhaps herself, that she had not sinned.

In the eyes of English law, the Council's deliberation and judgments are private matters, of no concern to courts or legislators as long as child custody and finances are not involved. In July 2008 Britain's highest justice, Lord Phillips, tried to make this clear. Echoing a statement made earlier that year by the archbishop of Canterbury, Rowan Williams, Phillips said that English law should recognize the right of Muslims, like everyone else, to settle personal affairs among themselves, in their case, according to sharia if they choose. The press pelted the archbishop for his speech; many commentators claimed that he had proposed introducing sharia law to England, and that mutilation, stoning, and the oppression of women were next on the English legal agenda. Six months later, Lord Phillips's comments elicited fewer responses—other news occupied the tabloids—but the press went on warning of judges adopting sharia and continues to do so today.

The English debate has also fueled concerns in the United States about the future of Western civilization. The *New York Times* paraphrased the conservative commentator Daniel Pipes's worries that "the United States stands to become another England or France, a place where Muslims are balkanized and ultimately threaten to impose sharia."[1] Although neither the archbishop nor the lord chief justice suggested incorporating rules of Islamic law into English law, their speeches left them open to charges that they would "recognize sharia." Some British Muslims, moreover, do call for the courts to turn over Muslims' marriage and divorce settlements to Islamic tribunals. As we shall see in the next chapter, the American movement to ban judges from applying sharia is partly inspired by the claim that English judges are already doing so.

Of all Western countries, Britain has the most developed set of institutions for Islamic dispute mediation.[2] Muslims can find Islamic tribunals in London, Birmingham, and elsewhere. The four or five major tribunals provide downloadable forms on their Web sites, charge set fees for service, and meet on scheduled days of the month. Most of them offer only nonbinding mediation. Each has its own characteristics: for example, the council in Birmingham's Central Mosque is led by women.

The existence and activities of these councils raise three important questions, which should bring into clearer relief what is, and is not, at stake in Islam's westward migration. First, why have these bodies developed more in England than elsewhere? Second, what do the sharia councils have to do with English law? Finally, do the councils, as often charged, perpetuate patriarchy?

MUSLIMS SETTLED IN GREAT BRITAIN IN A WAY that facilitated the eventual emergence of sharia-based institutions. Muslims are about 3 percent of the population. About half of the Muslims currently residing in Britain were born there; of the remaining half, most were born in Pakistan or Bangladesh. Moreover, many of the South Asians came from a few parts of Pakistani Kashmir and, from Bangladesh, Sylhet district. Until the mid-1960s, migration was mainly "circular"; that is, men came and worked and then went home, often to be replaced by someone else from the same village, frequently close kin. In England the men lived with others from the same lineage or who followed the same religious school. They thought of themselves as transient residents, and they regarded marriage and divorce as matters to be handled in the community overseas, with little or no involvement from the English courts.

British policies also encouraged the development of local institutions to handle family disputes. In the 1960s and 1970s the British government provided aid to local ethnic associations, which responded to Muslim demands about schooling, halal foods, and other religious practices. Muslims learned to resolve problems "in the community." Things changed in the late 1970s when state aid was severely curtailed, and mosques assumed greater local roles. By the late 1980s, and particularly after conflicts broke out over Salman Rushdie's book *The Satanic Verses*, Muslims came to see themselves as different because they were Muslims rather than because they were Pakistani or black. With deep divisions among British Muslims, calls for nationwide sharia never amounted to much. But locally, some Muslims turned to Islamic institutions as a way to keep private disputes in the community and proclaim allegiance to an increasingly beleaguered faith.

British traditions have looked kindly on religions as the source of moral guidance. As Archbishop Williams argued in 2008, when Muslims resolved matters by drawing on their own traditions, and as long as the outcomes did not conflict with prevailing laws, they were doing precisely what members of other faith communities regularly did. He challenged the notion that society could only be based on a single set of values, claiming instead that "our social identities are not constituted by one exclusive set of relations or mode of belonging."[3]

WHAT, THEN, DO THESE SHARIA COUNCILS HAVE to do with the law? Usually rather little because they act as mediators or they provide religious, nonlegal divorces. They occupy a niche that lies outside, or rather across, the civil law.

About half of British South Asian Muslims have transnational marriages, and many find difficulties in English civil courts if their marriages lead to divorce. Pakistan does not accept all English grounds for divorce, and England sometimes refuses to acknowledge Pakistani divorces, in particular where the husband has pronounced a unilateral divorce or *talaq*. Thus acquiring a religious divorce in England provides some assurance against harassment by irate (former) husbands or pesky judges in Pakistan or Bangladesh.

Other problems arise not from this sort of multi-state legal complexity but from confusions surrounding the relationships between civil law and religious practices in England. Many Muslim men and women think erroneously that an Islamic marriage in Britain makes them legally married. Others prefer to marry only in the Islamic fashion even though they know the law. Although churches legally register marriages, it has been difficult for mosques to achieve the same status—famously, more difficult than it has been for football stadiums, which have been used for mass marriages. In any case most Muslims prefer to marry at home.

Uncertain rules of equivalence across legal systems and ignorance of the laws at home and abroad: these and other obstacles have led many Muslims to avoid the civil law system entirely. Into this gap has stepped the extensive Islamic Sharia Council, the most noticeable of several Islamic tribunals and the group that gave Naseera her divorce. The Council operates from recently refurbished offices in a large house in a quiet residential area of Leyton in the eastern London suburbs. Most of its work concerns requests for Islamic divorces brought by women. The Council publishes the procedures to be followed in these cases on its Web site, and it can track the progress of any particular case on its computer database. Currently it logs about 600 cases each year.

A wife may approach a scholar in the Council and ask for her marriage to be dissolved. In many cases, the Council asks the husband if he would sign a talaq certificate (*talaq nama*); if he does so then the two have agreed to separate and the Council need take no action. He may have conditions, such as the return of the *mahr*, the marriage gift, forcing the Council to play a mediating role. In these cases it is the husband who freely decides to divorce, and who does divorce, and this action is referred to as a *khula*, a divorce by the husband at the request of the wife, and often with a payment from her. This leaves the majority of cases facing the Council, where the wife has asked for her marriage to be dissolved, and the husband either refuses to take action himself or fails to answer the Council's letters. In these cases the Council may decide to dissolve the marriage. A dissolution, or *faskh*, may be unconditional, or it may be conditional upon the wife returning the mahr. The scholars serving on the Council claim legitimacy to take such actions based on the argument that in lands without an Islamic legal system, scholars have a responsibility to provide this service. The scholars currently on the Council come from a variety of countries, have all lived for a long time in England, and represent a diversity of points of view on questions of *fiqh*, or Islamic jurisprudence. The Council also invites Muslims to come to the office to pose questions about their personal lives.

Women, then, are the main clients of the Council. They ask for divorce for many reasons. In a sample of 85 recent cases, most women mention a breakdown in the marriage because of irreconcilable differences, separation, or desertion; many also emphasize violence and abuse, and some claim the marriage was fraudulent or coerced. Most of the women and the men who went before the Council in the past four years were born in Pakistan or Bangladesh or are of South Asian ancestry, with Somalis the next largest category of petitioners. The women are much more likely to be born in Britain than are their husbands. The "modal" woman petitioner lives in England, is a British citizen of Pakistani or Bangladeshi origin (by birth or by ancestry), and requests divorce from a man who was born abroad and might still live abroad. In a considerable number of these cases, a woman living in Britain travels to Pakistan or Bangladesh and there marries a local man, whether on her initiative or at the command of her family.

In most cases where the petitioning wife meets the procedural requirements set by the Council, she receives a divorce. This is especially likely if she has obtained a civil divorce. The main issue, one that sometimes leads to lengthy debates among the councilors, involves the payment or return of the mahr promised or given by the husband to the wife. The mahr can be substantial, as much as several thousand pounds, and in those cases there may be protracted negotiations between the two parties.

The Council grants only an Islamic divorce but insists that a woman who married overseas or who registered her marriage in England obtain a civil divorce as well as a religious one. Although members of the Council may give advice about Islamic law on a range of matters, they do not pronounce on child custody or on the division of assets, knowing full well that if either party is dissatisfied with what they say they will ask the civil court for an order. From time to time a divorcing wife may ask a civil court to enforce her right to a specified amount of mahr or, more rarely, a husband may ask that wedding gifts be returned. Such cases are few and seldom reported, making it difficult to say much about them.

Despite occasional media efforts to raise alarms about these councils, the legal community by and large follows the lead of Lord Phillips, accepting them as reasonable conflict mediators. Judges understand that the councils make no civil law claims. Furthermore, judges may accept mediations as providing one among several bases for their rulings. In at least one recent case, the judge took an Islamic divorce pronounced by the Islamic Sharia council as having a legal effect, in that it triggered a preexisting agreement to repay mahr.[4] In this and other cases, English judges look for legal implications of agreements and decisions reached on sharia grounds, within the limits set by English law: that both parties freely agree to the outcome, that agreements are fair, and that children's best interests are guaranteed.[5]

ONE COULD ARGUE THAT EVEN IF THE SHARIA councils do not threaten anyone's legal rights, even if they mainly provide a service valued by women petitioners, and even if they fit relatively well into the English religious and legal landscape, nonetheless they foster patriarchy because they bring to bear a set of rules and a cultural background that are imbued with notions of male superiority. These attitudes must lead to decisions that disfavor women.

But is this true?

It certainly is true that some of the older South Asian councilors speak in a way that some younger, British-born women dislike. But the wave of the future might be better seen in a second sharia council that meets once or twice a month in Birmingham's Central Mosque. The Birmingham Sharia Council developed from a women's crisis center begun by Wageha Syeda, a Muslim woman and medical doctor. Because many women who sought Syeda's advice wished to divorce their husbands, in 2005 she asked the Birmingham Central Mosque to sponsor a body that could oversee Islamic divorces. Among the four scholars who were asked to join the council was a woman, Amra Bone.

In sessions of the Council that I attended in 2011, three women took charge of sessions. Bone opened the sessions and then asked her male colleagues if they had further questions or opinions. Syeda usually had more contact with petitioners prior to the sessions and would add background. A third woman acted as the Council's administrator and prepared the agenda and briefs for the councilors. Two older men completed the Council's panel.

In one case heard in July 2011, Bone welcomed the petitioner, a Birmingham-area woman who, accompanied by her father, had come to request an Islamic divorce. The couple had married in Pakistan and, after living in Britain, the husband recently returned there. The petitioner claimed that her husband neglected her and in any event could not father children. They had approached the Council office a few months earlier and said they were not going to bother with a civil divorce, but were advised that, because the husband had entered Britain on a work visa, they were obliged to do so. Now civil divorce was underway. This upset Bone and the others a bit because they do not like to grant a religious divorce before the civil procedure is done. "You must complete the civil divorce; civil law is supreme here," Bone told the petitioner. But they decided to grant the religious divorce in any case, because the petitioner had come to them first. They decided that the husband's failure to support his wife, and his decision to return to Pakistan, justified a decision to separate them by means of *tafriq*, a judicially enforced divorce. As Bone then explained to the woman's father, even though the woman could have just remarried without coming to them, "not everyone is aware of how sharia works. If you marry again some people will ask you if you got a divorce from a sharia council. It is a good idea to have it; you have to consider how society sees you."

Bone and Syeda regularly gave the petitioner practical advice: "register your marriage next time," "join a gym and make yourself healthier." The manner in which they welcomed the women (and, less often, the men) made it clear that the Council was mainly there to advise women and help them to move on with their lives, within an Islamic framework.

Indeed, it may be precisely because British Muslim women face substantial social and economic problems that this sort of sharia council—as well as the male-dominated one in London—is needed. Muslim women from South Asia have the least education, highest unemployment, and highest suicide rates of any demographic group in the United Kingdom. They, like their non-Muslim South Asian counterparts, are supposed to uphold family honor. Forced marriage remains a real problem, even for educated women. Arranged marriages may work out, but when, as in Naseera's case, they pair a well-educated British woman with an uneducated Pakistani cousin, divorce is not unlikely. And it is here that sharia, as interpreted by councils, may provide an element of social and moral support for those women who seek a divorce. The sharia councils require that wives get civil divorces as well as religious ones, unless they were married only in Islamic fashion in Britain. They thus push women toward the justice system, not away from it.

ENGLAND HAS THE MOST DEVELOPED SET OF sharia-based tribunals. Their growing prominence provides three important lessons to other countries in Western Europe and North America.

First, the English case highlights the importance of contracts within Islam. Marriage in Islam is a contract, not a sacrament. British Muslims generally conduct religious marriages at home, not in the mosque, and they may or may not also register with the state so as to become legally married. Divorce is essentially the recognition that the contract has been broken.

Rather than see this Islamic logic as threatening the civil state, we can see it as the basis for constructing bridges between Islamic and Western systems. For example, some Islamic scholars in England and elsewhere in Europe argue that because a civil marriage also is a contract—you need consent, witnesses, and written proof of the event—it is enough to constitute an Islamic marriage, no mosque or imam or Arabic utterances needed.

Many of these scholars also argue that, by the same token, civil divorce is sufficient to break the Islamic contract and that therefore there is really no need for sharia councils to grant Islamic divorces. This argument is the majority view among French Islamic scholars and those in some other European countries. Bone made this point at the Birmingham Council when she told the petitioner that her civil divorce was sufficient from an Islamic point of view, though she felt that obtaining an Islamic divorce certificate remained a good idea in case others in her community considered civil divorce inadequate. The certificates also reduce the likelihood of legal troubles in case of remarriage in Islamic-law countries. The sharia councils go further by insisting in the case of a legal marriage that a civil divorce proceeding be underway before an Islamic divorce will be issued. Only with a civil proceeding, they say, are the legal rights of the parties protected.

Conversely, some European jurists argue that Islamic divorce proceedings in, say, Morocco or Pakistan can effectively meet the conditions for a divorce by mutual consent and thus should be recognized on a case-by-case basis. So the contract model seems to offer a way to bring socio-legal communities together.

Second, the experience of the sharia councils

shows that even with a maximally developed system of religious mediation, the line between religious bodies and the civil law remains clear. English courts will not delegate their authority to a mediation body; they always will look at the facts of a case and decide what is fair and reasonable according to English law. As Justice Peter Singer of the High Family Court explained to me in 2008:

> We are very paternalistic on money, likely to say 'that's not fair' even if the wife has agreed to it. This is not an area of contractual certainty; the adults are not competent to bind the court, and the courts will be reluctant to agree to a settlement where the wife surrenders her right to come back and ask for maintenance, or for more maintenance, at a later stage, should conditions change.

The justice was even more categorical when children were in question: all agreements, even those signed under a solicitor's aegis, are inspected to see whether they meet the best interests of the child. I have interviewed dozens of family-law lawyers and judges and have yet to find a single instance where a judge recognized the result of a sharia council mediation as having legal relevance. This is not surprising considering that the London Council has given up providing formal guidance on matters that could go to court.

Third, the English experience suggests that religious women's interests can best be protected by encouraging the use of civil institutions alongside religious ones, not by restricting the exercise of religious freedom. As Anne Phillips suggests in *Multiculturalism without Culture* (2007), we ought to focus not on restricting the capacities of Muslims to seek religious divorces but on providing resources and information about the range of available legal and social assistance.[6] Instead of cutting off venues, help people with informed venue shopping. In the Islamic legal world, tribunals offer women a religious good not otherwise obtainable (and in this respect Muslim women have an advantage over Orthodox Jewish women, whose husbands must agree to divorce). The tribunals afford one way to broker the confusing and often incoherent world of international private law, making it easier for some Muslims to get on with family life. And tribunals provide an open and institutionalized framework to encourage a convergence of Islamic norms with English law. Ultimately, it is in this sense that we ought to understand the calls by the archbishop and Lord Phillips to "recognize sharia."

What about elsewhere? Would something like the English sharia tribunals fit into the social and legal frameworks of other societies in Europe and in North America? Consider the reasons why they flourish in England: strong ties between societies in South Asia and in England, long-standing practices of finding community-based solutions to problems, and a mainstream legal culture accepting of such solutions, within limits.

We would expect to find such tribunals in the United States, with its similar legal tradition, but mainly in those spheres where Muslim communities have preserved strong ties with countries of origin. This seems to be the case: Islamic tribunals act on requests for divorce in several U.S. cities, and the tribunals tend to involve scholars from South Asia. In Canada tribunals were proposed for Ontario but met loud resistance from other Muslims, in part because they were not, as is the case in England, based on preexisting community practices of mediation. We would, correctly, expect them to be least imaginable in France, where the law is supposed to send messages about shared values. Marrying outside state institutions there is an abandonment of one's duties as a citizen, and performing a religious marriage before a civil one can land you in jail.

Whether you see Islamic tribunals as offering valuable services to members of a religious community, or as threatening to divide citizens and override common values, is largely a matter of how you weigh competing political goods. England seems to be moving toward a balance of increasingly active Islamic tribunals and vigilant judges policing the boundaries of acceptable settlements. Against the deep English historical background of religious freedom for dissenting Protestants, community-based movements for civil rights, and transnationally oriented Muslims, this balance makes sense. The English path may become a model for others less in its substance than in the reasonable fashion in which public figures attempt a compromise among competing political values.

4

Off-Target:
U.S. Anti-Sharia Campaigns

Since November 2010 legislators in twenty or so states have passed or proposed bills banning sharia.[1] Oklahoma led the charge when voters massively supported a state constitutional amendment banning state courts from "considering or using" either international law or sharia law. State Representative Rex Duncan said he was motivated to sponsor the measure—which was put on hold by a federal judge until hearings could be held on its constitutionality—after learning of a New Jersey judge who enforced sharia and because of the "cancer" of sharia spreading in Britain. He added, "There is no logical reason why a court would look to the law of France or Saudi Arabia."

Actually, there are a number of logical reasons why a judge would do exactly that. If a judge in Virginia is to decide whether to enforce a contract or accept a divorce decision made in France or in Saudi Arabia, he or she has to look to the laws of that country. The Virginia judge must decide whether the contract or divorce was carried out in accordance with those laws, what the reasonable expectations of the parties to the case would be in those countries, and whether any aspect of the foreign law violated the laws of Virginia or of the United States. A Saudi Arabian law might contain terms that derive from Islam, just as American laws might contain terms that derive from Christianity, but the Virginia judge looks only to the duly enacted laws of that country, whatever their inspiration or origin, not to religious beliefs or texts. Even in hyper-secularist France, judges do precisely this when considering cases involving laws inspired by religious doctrine.

It is thus normal and indeed unavoidable that from time to time U.S. judges decide whether the ruling of a foreign court should be acknowledged in the United States or whether a contract signed overseas should be enforced here. In a country with Islamic elements in its legal codes—and there are many such countries, from Indonesia to Morocco—some of those decisions or contracts that U.S. judges scrutinize will contain elements derived from Islam. Are American judges doing anything more than this? Do their judgments demonstrate the perversion of American justice by sharia, as the sponsors of anti-sharia legislation claim?

Let us consider the strongest case for alarm so far: a detailed report issued in May 2011 by the neo-conservative Center for Security Policy. The CSP concludes, "Sharia law *has* entered into state court decisions, in conflict with the Constitution and state public policy."[2] The thorough, 635-page document now has become the touchstone for those claiming that U.S. courts apply sharia law.

The document leads off with its "top 20 cases." Though selected to exhibit the danger of creeping sharia, they seem to involve American judges applying

American laws. In thirteen of them, the judge had to decide whether to accept a decision made in a foreign court. The judges made their decisions based on U.S. jurisprudence, and appellate courts either affirmed or overturned those decisions. Of the remaining seven cases, four concern the enforceability of an Islamic marriage contract and were decided according to standard U.S. contract law; one involves the question of whether binding arbitration may be carried out by a mosque-affiliated body (the court said yes); one debates whether a court may enforce a dispute between an imam and his mosque board involving the content of his sermons (the court said no); and one, the most controversial of the lot, asks whether a man's religious beliefs are germane to the question of his criminal liability.

If these most egregious cases do not create a cause for concern, it is unlikely that others will. Let us look a little closer at how the judges reasoned.

Some of the contract cases featured in the report involved marriage payments. For example, in

In re marriage of Obaidi, a court in Washington State enforced a contract according to which the husband had agreed to pay his wife $20,000 as a marriage gift (*mahr*). The appellate court overturned the ruling on grounds that the husband could not be said to have consented to the agreement because he was unable to read the language in which the contract was written. Sensible decision, it would seem. Why did the case make the "top 20" list? Because the trial court referred to the fact that mahr was an element in an Islamic marriage, and for the CSP this is evidence that sharia has "entered into state court decisions."

This conclusion is unwarranted; the judge applied American legal principles.

In *Hosain v. Malik*, one of the few cases where the CSP wants us to find the appellate outcome troubling, a Maryland trial judge upheld a Pakistani court ruling that had granted custody of a child to the father. The decision was upheld on appeal. The debate on the appellate level concerned whether the Pakistani court had based its decision on the best interests of the child, which is the applicable American judicial principle. The court's majority decided that the Pakistani court had indeed done so.

Regardless of whether one agrees with the Pakistani judges or the Americans who upheld their decision—and neither I nor the CSP could second-guess the trial judge without access to the original materials and testimony—the legal issue facing the Maryland court was a familiar one: did the foreign court apply the appropriate Maryland (and general U.S.) legal test in awarding custody? The judges' reasoning had nothing to do with sharia; they would have asked the same question had the original decision been made in Germany or Chile.

In some cases the court refused to take action on grounds that doing so would involve excessive entanglement with religion in violation of the First Amendment, as in a case where both levels of Arkansas jurisdiction rejected a suit brought against a mosque because to take the case would have meant making a ruling about the appropriate content for sermons. The court thought that doing so would be crossing into dangerous territory, just as other courts have concluded regarding Jewish marriage law or Christian church regulations. You might think the CSP would applaud this stance, but because the court referred to Islam in *rejecting* the suit, the case made the danger list.

Far from the worst offenders, these cases actually show that the multi-tiered structure of the U.S. judicial system produces results that should satisfy even the most strongly anti-Islamic observers. In fourteen of the twenty cases, the appellate court decided in a way that presumably even the CSP would have wanted, in that it rejected a decision by a court in an Islamic country, or found invalid a contract that drew on religious sources. In the six other cases, the CSP disliked the outcome because the courts at both levels affirmed either a court decision of a country that has Islamic elements in its laws, or the U.S. courts upheld a contract between two Muslims that was inspired by their shared Islamic faith and also met

U.S. legal standards. However, in *all* these cases, the courts were applying American law.

Such is true even of the one case that, at the trial level, could be seen as making an unwise reference to Islamic beliefs, a case that proponents of the Oklahoma ballot measure cited as justification for their proposal. In this New Jersey case (*S.D. v. M.J.R.*) the trial court judge ruled that a husband did not have criminal intent when he forced himself sexually on his wife because he believed that he had the right to do so. He knew that his wife did not consent to sex, but he thought that he was in his rights as a Muslim to have sex anyway. (This judge did find the man guilty of other criminal acts against his wife.)

The decision was overturned on appeal. CSP and others claim that the trial judge had excused the man because he was following Islamic law. The judge's reasoning was misguided, but not in the way these critics claim. As the appellate court pointed out in overturning the lower court's decision, the judge was wrong because he thought New Jersey law required that the husband have criminal intent in order to be found guilty of a crime and that to have criminal intent meant he knew what he did was wrong. This is a mistaken reading of the law; it suffices that he knew his wife did not consent to sex but proceeded anyway, thus forcing himself on her. What counts as a "crime" is to be found in New Jersey statutes, not the mind of the perpetrator. The trial judge's reasoning was not based on sharia; it was based on his erroneous assumption that the husband's beliefs about acceptable behavior had legal implications.

I agree with CSP and the legislators fearful of sharia that judges in the United States should not apply sharia; nor should English judges, as I have written elsewhere.[3] Most American Muslims would agree as well. Judges working in the United States should apply the laws that are valid in the United States, and that is precisely what they do, even in the cases that supposedly prove the contrary. The laws of the United States and of all the states allow people—whether Christian, Muslim, or none-of-the-above—to enter into contracts such as those governing mahr. Those laws also allow people to submit disputes to private parties for arbitration. Furthermore, they authorize U.S. courts to recognize as legally valid (or not, depending on the facts) the procedures and findings of foreign courts, within the limits mentioned above.[4]

What *is* alarming is not how judges make their decisions, but how politicians seek to win votes by singling out Muslims for suspicion. If people can be made to think that judges are already duped by Muslims into applying sharia, then they may view Muslims and Islam as all the more dangerous, as a fifth column in America trying to subvert our way of life. For Americans who are uncomfortable with changes in their communities—new people, new kinds of buildings, new religions—creeping sharia provides a useful scapegoat that seems to provide moral justification for opposition to mosques, Muslim schools, and even religiously appropriate dress.

Afterword:
Principles and Pragmatics

Underneath the rhetoric of Islam-bashing and sharia scares, we see everyday sanity. The confrontations in Murfreesboro betrayed ignorance and fear, but they also brought out non-Muslims who defended the rights of Muslims to exercise religious freedom. These ordinary Americans defended the Constitution and argued the practical case for allowing local Muslims a larger mosque.

In France, Germany, and Britain, politicians publicly pretend that multiculturalism caused current social ills, but at the same time, most also seek workable solutions to real problems: finding new spaces for prayer (France), trying to get rival Muslim factions to talk (Germany), encouraging the mosques to work with the police for their common interests (Britain). In all these cases, political leaders realize that the best route toward integration is the one already pursued for other sub-national religious groups, and some also see that their own national traditions demand that Muslims be treated like those of other faiths with respect to their religious beliefs and religious needs. Sanity is even invading Web sites. The phony demographics once proclaimed on most anti-Islam Web sites—Muslims will take over Europe in 50 years!—have faded as real demographic information arrives and is broadcast widely.

Blaming Islam will retain its appeal, however, as long as Islam continues to be perceived as alien, a foreign source of non-Western values. Islam has become a major, visible religious presence in Western Europe and North America only relatively recently. While many third- and fourth-generation Muslims live in Britain or the United States, Islamic leaders remain mostly foreign-born. Few, if any, internationally credible Muslim theologians or jurists have been trained in the West. Many major cities still do not have mosques large enough to accommodate demands for prayer. Schools and universities are still in development. This process will take time, and as it does, Islam will retain some of its foreign character.

Those are the challenges facing Muslims interested in developing and adapting Islam to their new countries. Those of us who have lived in the West longer face different challenges: holding fast to our principles of equality and liberty, and persuading others to do the same.

Notes

Introduction

[1] Here I agree with Timothy Garton Ash's comments: http://www.guardian.co.uk/commentisfree/2011/jul/29/internet-norway-killer-censorship-folly.

[2] See the CNN program on the controversy: http://www.cnn.com/2011/US/studentnews/03/24/unwelcome.muslims.next.door.guide/index.html.

Chapter 1

[1] On the debate following Merkel's speech, see *Der Spiegel*: http://www.spiegel.de/international/germany/0,1518,723702,00.html; on Cameron's speech, see *The Guardian*: http://www.guardian.co.uk/politics/2011/feb/05/david-cameron-attack-multicultur-

alism-coalition; for Sarkozy's speech see *National Post*: http://
www.nationalpost.com/news/Multiculturalism+clearly+failure
+Sarkozy/4261825/story.html.

[2] A useful summary of the story of immigration and integration
in these countries is in Joel S. Fetzer and J. Christopher Soper,
Muslims and the State in Britain, France, and Germany. Cambridge: Cambridge University Press, 2005.

[3] See *The Economist*'s analysis: http://www.economist.com/
node/17469563.

[4] Olivier Roy, *Globalized Islam*, New York: Columbia University
Press, 2004; Marc Sageman, *Leaderless Jihad*. Philadelphia: University of Pennsylvania Press, 2008.

[5] Bhikhu Parekh, *Rethinking Multiculturalism*. Cambridge, MA:
Harvard University Press, 2002.

[6] See Claude Guéant, "Non à la France des commautarismes" and
Sylvain Cypel, "Communautarisme, affaires et procès," *Le Monde*,
March 16, 2010, for the citations in this paragraph and the next.

[7] These facts do not deter French politicians from continuing to
make such remarks, as when, in a televised debate on September
28, 2011, Montfermeil Mayor Xavier Lemoine explained to his
stunned interviewer that the idea of a "right to a difference" was
the cause of the absence of state services in his poor community. See the video clip: http://www.youtube.com/watch?v=C-
62oHDI67Y.

[8] See John R. Bowen, *Why the French Don't Like Headscarves*.
Princeton: Princeton University Press, 2006. For a comparison
of French and German policies see *Riva Kastoryano, Negotiating
Identities*. Princeton: Princeton University Press, 2002.

[9] For an overview of the Dutch story, see Ian Buruma, *Murder in Amsterdam*. New York: Penguin, 2006.

[10] J.W. Duyvendak and P.W.A. Scholten, "Beyond National Models of Integration. The Coproduction of Integration Policy Frames in the Netherlands," *Journal of International Migration and Integration*, 12 (3): 331–48, 2011; Peter Van der Veer, "Pim Fortuyn, Theo van Gogh, and the politics of tolerance in the Netherlands," *Public Culture* 18(1): 111–124, 2006.

Chapter 2

[1] Christopher Caldwell, *Reflections on the Revolution in Europe*. New York: Doubleday, 2009.

[2] Paul M. Sniderman and Louk Hagendoorn, *When Ways of Life Collide*. Princeton: Princeton University Press, 2007.

[3] For a brief account of the study, see: http://vorige.nrc.nl/international/article2064610.ece/Gay_attackers_usually_young_Dutch_men.

[4] "Gallup Coexist Index 2009: A Global Study of Interfaith Relations": http://www.cmes.lu.se/wp-content/uploads/2009/10/the-gallup-coexist-index-2009.pdf; The Pew Forum on Religion & Public Life, "U.S. Religious Landscape Survey," 2009: http://religions.pewforum.org/reports#.

[5] Ibid, "Gallup Coexist Index 2009."

[6] Pew Research Center, Forum on Religion & Public Life, "The Future of the Global Muslim Population, 2011": http://pewforum.org/future-of-the-global-muslim-population-main-factors-fertility.aspx.

[7] The Pew study projects differences between TFR for Muslims and non-Muslims to fall from 0.7 to 0.4 by 2030 for Europe as a whole, and for France from 0.8 to 0.5: http://pewforum.org/future-of-the-global-muslim-population-regional-europe.aspx.

[8] Ibid.

[9] Sageman, *Leaderless Jihad*, p. 60.

Chapter 3

[1] Andrea Elliott, "Critics cost Muslim educator her dream school," *The New York Times*, April 28, 2008. See: http://www.nytimes.com/2008/04/28/nyregion/28school.html.

[2] I speak of England regarding law because laws and jurisdictions in England and Wales are distinct from those of Scotland and Northern Ireland.

[3] Rowan Williams, "Civil and Religious Law in England: a religious perspective," *The Guardian*, February 7, 2008 (emphasis in original). See http://www.guardian.co.uk/uk/2008/feb/07/religion.world2.

[4] John R. Bowen, "How Could English Courts Recognize Shariah?" *St. Thomas Law Review*, 7 (3): 411–35, 2011.

[5] One body, the Muslim Arbitration Tribunal, located in Nuneaton in the Midlands, does sometimes carry out legally binding arbitration, but only in commercial matters. One cannot legally subject a marriage or divorce to binding arbitration in England. See Bowen, "How Could English Courts Recognize Shariah?"

[6] Anne Phillips, *Multiculturalism without Culture*. Princeton: Princeton University Press, 2007.

Chapter 4

[1] Readers can follow these efforts at http://jurist.org/paper-chase/2011/09/federal-appeals-court-considers-oklahoma-sharia-law-ban.php. Each state's wording is a bit different; some, such as Arizona, strive for constitutionality by targeting "religious sectarianism" rather than sharia.

[2] Center for Security Policy, "Shariah Law and American State Courts," p. 8: http://shariahinamericancourts.com/wp-content/uploads/2011/06/Shariah_Law_And_American_State_Courts_1.4_06212011.pdf, accessed September 2011. Case summaries and reports are taken from the CSP report.

[3] Bowen, "How Could English Courts Recognize Shariah?"

[4] Relevant to this question, but ignored by the anti-sharia studies, is the 1983 New York State law that allows the state to prevent a civil divorce if a Jewish husband has not provided his wife with a religious divorce, the get. Though framed in neutral language, the statute does constitute a civil intervention into a religious procedure, similar to the English provision mentioned in Chapter 4.

ABOUT THE AUTHOR

JOHN R. BOWEN is Dunbar-Van Cleve Professor in the Department of Anthropology at Washington University in St. Louis. His books include *A New Anthropology of Islam*, *Can Islam Be French?*, *Why the French Don't Like Headscarves*, and *Islam, Law and Equality in Indonesia*.

BOSTON REVIEW BOOKS

Boston Review Books is an imprint of *Boston Review*, a bimonthly magazine of ideas. The book series, like the magazine, covers a lot of ground. But a few premises tie it all together: that democracy depends on public discussion; that sometimes understanding means going deep; that vast inequalities are unjust; and that human imagination breaks free from neat political categories. Visit bostonreview.net for more information.